L
n
d
o
Y
a
L
K
H
L
P.
O
P.

T
p
(*
M
H
G
Ju
D
D
I

Utopia – *Voyage*, *Shipwreck* and *Salvage*.

PIRANDELLO'S
Henry IV

a new version by
TOM STOPPARD

faber and faber

First published in 2004
by Faber and Faber Limited
3 Queen Square London WC1N 3AU

Typeset by Country Setting, Kingsdown, Kent CT14 8ES
Printed in England by Mackays of Chatham plc, Chatham, Kent

A CIP record for this book
is available from the British Library

ISBN
0–571–22507–1

2 4 6 8 10 9 7 5 3 1

Pirandello's **Henry IV**, in this version by Tom Stoppard, was first performed at the Donmar Warehouse on 29 April 2004. The cast in order of appearance was as follows:

Landolf James Lance
Harold Stuart Burt
Ordulf Neil McDermott
Bertold Nitzan Sharron
Giovanni Brian Poyser
Di Nolli Orlando Wells
Belcredi David Yelland
Doctor Robert Demeger
Matilda Francesca Annis
Frida Tania Emery
Henry Ian McDiarmid

Director Michael Grandage
Designer Christopher Oram
Lighting Designer Neil Austin
Music and Sound Score Adam Cork
Sound Designer Fergus O'Hare

Characters

Landolf
Harold
Ordulf
Bertold
attendants to Henry IV

Giovanni
an elderly manservant

Di Nolli
a young count, 'Henry's' nephew

Belcredi
a baron, Matilda's consort

Genoni
a doctor

Matilda
a countess

Frida
Matilda's daughter, engaged to Di Nolli

'Henry IV'
Holy Roman Emperor

HENRY IV

Act One

The Throne Room. There are two full-length, life-size modern portraits, of a young man and a young woman dressed as Henry IV and Matilda, Countess of Tuscany. Harold, Landolf, Ordulf and Bertold – wearing the · costumes of eleventh-century German knights – enter.

Landolf Next – the throne room!

Harold The throne room of the Emperor's Palace at Goslar!

Ordulf Or could be Hartzburg . . .

Harold . . . or Worms, depending.

Landolf Depending on where we are in the story – he keeps us on the hop.

Ordulf Saxony . . .

Harold Lombardy . . .

Landolf The Rhine . . .

Ordulf Keep your voice down.

Landolf He's asleep.

Bertold Hang about. I'm confused. I thought we were doing *Henry IV*.

Landolf So?

Bertold Well, this place, these get-ups – it's not him.

Ordulf Who?

3

Bertold The King of France, Henry IV.

Landolf Whoops.

Ordulf He thought it was the French one.

Landolf Wrong country, mate, wrong century, wrong Henry.

Harold It's the German Henry IV, Salian Dynasty.

Ordulf The Holy Roman Emperor.

Landolf The Canossa one – walked to Canossa to get absolution from the Pope. Church v. State, that's the game round here, day in, day out.

Ordulf Emperor at home to Pope –

Harold Pope away to Anti-Pope –

Landolf King away to Anti-King –

Ordulf Like war with Saxony –

Harold Plus with revolting barons –

Landolf His own kids . . .

Bertold Now I know why I've been feeling wrong in these clothes, these are not your French 1580s.

Harold Forget the 1580s.

Ordulf Think the ten-hundreds.

Landolf Work it out, if Canossa was January 1077 . . .

Bertold I'm fucked.

Ordulf Royally.

Bertold I've been reading up the wrong . . .

Landolf Sad. We're four hundred years behind you. Ahead of you. You're not even a twinkle in our eye.

Bertold (*angered*) You got any idea how much stuff I read about Henry IV of France in the last two weeks?

Harold Didn't you know Tony was our Adalbert, Bishop of Bremen?

Bertold What Adalbert? – No one told me anything!

Landolf Well, when Tony died, at first the young Count –

Bertold The Count Di Nolli? He's the one. Why didn't he tell me?

Landolf – first he thought the three of us would do. Then Himself started moaning – 'They've driven out Adalbert!' – he didn't realise 'Adalbert' had died on us, he thought the Bishops of Cologne and Mainz had booted him out, Tony I mean, all clear so far?

Bertold Wait. Bishop Tony of what?

Ordulf You're fucked.

Harold Forget the bishops. The bishops are not the problem, the problem is we don't know who you are.

Bertold So what am I playing?

Ordulf Um, Bertold.

Bertold Bertold who? Why Bertold?

Landolf Himself kept yelling, 'They've driven out Adalbert, so get me Bertold! I want Bertold!'

Harold We eyeballed each other – who dat?

Landolf Never heard of him.

Ordulf And here you are.

Landolf You'll be great.

Bertold No, I won't, which way's out?

5

Harold No, no, relax.

Landolf This'll cheer you up – we don't know who we are either. He's Harold, he's Ordulf, I'm Landolf, that's what he calls us so that's who we are, you get used to it, but it's a puppet show. Who are we really? . . . Just names of the period. Same with you, I suppose, Bertold. Tony was the only one with a proper character, the Bishop of Bremen. He was a good bishop, too, God rest him.

Harold Always reading himself up.

Landolf And he bossed Himself about, not himself, Himself, His Majesty, he was like his teacher. With us, we're his Privy Counsellors but we're only here to take up space. It's in the books – the barons had it in for Henry for surrounding himself with young bloods not quite premier league, so that's us. Royal hangers-on, do anything for him, like a drink, a few laughs . . .

Bertold Laughs?

Harold Just do what we do.

Ordulf It's not as easy as it looks.

Landolf Bit of a waste, really. We've got the scenery, we've got the costumes, we could put on proper shows, history's always popular, and there's enough stuff in Henry IV for several tragedies. But us four – we're stranded, nobody gives us our moves, nothing to act, it's that old form-without-content. We're worse off than the real ones. They were given sod-all to play, true, but they didn't know that, so they just did what they did because that's what they did. Life. Which means, look after number one. They sold titles and stuff. And here we are, great outfits, handsome surroundings, shame about the puppets.

6

Harold No, fair do's, you have to be ready to come out with the right answer or you're in trouble.

Landolf Yeh, that's true.

Bertold Well, that's it, innit? How'm I supposed to give him the right answer when I've been learning the wrong Henry?

Harold You'll have to put that right, right off.

Ordulf We'll all pitch in.

Harold There's lots of stuff on him, a quick skim will do you for now.

Harold Here's one . . . who's the skirt, do you know?

Bertold (*looking*) Her? Well, spot the deliberate mistake . . . she doesn't belong for a start, a modern picture like that . . .

Harold You're not wrong, you're right.

Landolf But here's the thing – it's only a mistake if you think of them as paintings.

Bertold Which is what they are.

Landolf They are and they aren't. To Himself, seeing as he never touches them –

Bertold So what are they to him?

Landolf This is just my theory but I bet I'm right – to him they're more like whatsits, representations of – yes – what you'd see in a mirror. That one is him just as he is, same clothes, in this throne room, which is right in every detail, no surprises. If it was a mirror, you'd see yourself in the eleventh century. So that's what *he* sees. Himself. So it's like mirrors reflecting back a world which comes to life in them, like it will for you, you'll see, don't worry.

7

Bertold Don't worry?

Harold It's a laugh.

Bertold So how did you get to be so into it . . .?

Landolf Over nine hundred years of experience.

Ordulf Take your cue from us.

Bertold What about this other one – the Emperor's wife?

Harold Not at all. His wife is Bertha of Susa, sister of Amadeus II of Savoy.

Ordulf He can't stand her. He wants to dump her. He likes being one of the lads, like us.

Landolf This one here is his sworn enemy – Matilda, the Countess of Tuscany.

Harold The one who put the Pope up.

Landolf At Canossa.

Ordulf Pope Gregory VII. We hate him. You're on. Go out there an unknown, come back a star. Let's go.

> *They brace themselves to go 'onstage', move to exit, but Giovanni enters, in modern dress.*

Giovanni (*hurried and anxious*) Hey . . . psst – Franco! Lolo!

Harold What's up?

Bertold Hey. What's he doing here?

Landolf Wrong century – get out!

Ordulf (*larking about*) Get thee hence! – emissary of Gregory VII!

Harold Be gone!

Giovanni Leave off!

Ordulf 'Tis forbidden!

Harold This be sorcery!

Landolf (*to Bertold*) A spirit conjured up by the Wizard of Rome! Quick, draw your sword.

Giovanni (*yelling*) Stop taking the piss. The young Count has arrived . . . with a party . . .

Landolf Ah! Great! Any women?

Ordulf Good looking?

Giovanni There's two gentlemen.

Harold What about the women?

Giovanni The Countess and her daughter.

Landolf (*surprised*) Oh! – how come?

Ordulf The Countess?

Giovanni That's right – the Countess.

Landolf (*to Bertold*) Her daughter is engaged to the young Count.

Harold And the men?

Giovanni I don't know them.

Harold (*to Bertold*) Well, that'll introduce a bit of content.

Ordulf Messengers from the Pope – this is more like it.

Giovanni Will you let me tell you?

Harold Go on, then.

Giovanni I think one's a doctor.

Landolf Oh, right, another doctor.

Harold (*to Bertold*) You brought us luck!

Landolf Watch us work the doctor.

Bertold I think I'm out of my depth.

Giovanni Listen – they want to come in.

Landolf Here? *She* can't come in here.

Harold Now that would be content.

Landolf We'd have a real tragedy on our hands.

Bertold Why's that?

Ordulf (*pointing at the portrait*) It's *her*, don't you see?

Harold What do they want in here?

Ordulf If Himself sees her he'll blow his lid.

Landolf That's if he still knows her.

Giovanni If he wakes up, you're to keep him out.

Ordulf Oh, easy! – and how're we supposed to do that?

Giovanni Bloody hell – use force if you have to. I've been told – get on with it.

Harold He could already be awake.

Ordulf Let's go.

Landolf Tell us later what's going on.

Giovanni Lock the door and take the key out.

> *Landolf, Harold, Ordulf and Bertold leave. Di Nolli comes in.*

Di Nolli All clear?

Giovanni Yes, My Lord.

*Di Nolli exits for a moment to invite the others in.
The first to enter is Baron Tito Belcredi, followed by
Doctor Dionisio Genoni, then Countess Matilda and
her daughter Frida. Giovanni bows and exits. Matilda
is about forty-five years old; she is still beautiful
although she repairs the inevitable damage with heavy
but expert make-up. Belcredi is lean, prematurely
grizzled, slightly younger. Frida is nineteen. She's
engaged to the young Count Carlo Di Nolli, a stiff
young man in full mourning. They enter nervously,
looking at the room with curiosity (except for Di
Nolli) and almost whispering to begin with.*

Belcredi Incredible . . .

Doctor Fascinating! The dementia carried through to the
last detail.

Matilda Ah, there it is. Yes, yes . . . Look at it . . . My
God . . . Frida, look . . .

Frida Oh, your portrait!

Matilda No. Look. It's not me, it's you.

Di Nolli What did I tell you?

Matilda But it's uncanny! Look, Frida – can't you see it's
you?

Frida Well . . . really I . . .

Matilda Look, Tito.

Belcredi Wouldn't dream of it, on principle.

Matilda Idiot! He thinks he's being gall-ant. You tell her,
Doctor.

Belcredi Psst – Doctor – for pity's sake – don't get
involved in this.

Doctor In what?

Matilda Ignore him. He's insufferable.

Frida He plays the fool for his supper, didn't you know?

Belcredi Watch where you put your feet!

Doctor Why?

Belcredi You're wearing hobnailed boots.

Doctor Really?

Belcredi And you're about to step on somebody's toes.

Doctor Oh . . . come on . . . what's so strange about a daughter looking like her mother?

Belcredi Crunch, too late!

Matilda Why, what did he say?

Doctor Nothing special.

Belcredi He said there was nothing strange about it. In which case, why did you act so stunned?

Matilda (*enraged*) For the very reason that the resemblance is so natural – fool! – because that's my portrait and to see my daughter looking back at me was an amazing thing, so I was amazed – all right? – and you can keep your insinuations to yourself.

    Embarrassed silence.

Frida Oh God, it always ends in a row.

Belcredi (*apologetically*) I wasn't insinuating anything. I just happened to notice you didn't share your mother's amazement. If you were surprised at anything, it was at your mother being amazed.

Matilda Well, obviously! She didn't know me when I was her age. But I saw myself, and saw I was . . . just like she is now.

Doctor No more than one would expect. Because for the daughter it's just a picture, a moment caught and complete in itself . . . while for the mother it brings back a whole life – how she moved, gestured, smiled, spoke, everything which isn't in the painting . . .

Matilda Exactly.

Doctor . . . all sprung to life in your daughter.

Matilda Thank you! But when I speak as I feel, he has to go and spoil it to annoy me.

Doctor (*continues in his professional tone, turning to Belcredi*) Resemblance, you see, my dear Baron, often resides where you least expect it – which is how . . .

Belcredi Which is how some people might even find a resemblance between you and me.

Di Nolli Please, please, we've got off the point.

Frida That's what happens when he's around.

Matilda Which is exactly why I didn't want him to come.

Belcredi How ungrateful, after all the fun you have at my expense.

Di Nolli Tito, I beg you – enough. The Doctor is here, we have serious business and you know how important it is to me.

Doctor Good. Let's make a start by getting a few things clear. How did this portrait come to be here? Did you give it to him back at the beginning?

Matilda No, how would I? I was just a girl – like Frida – not even engaged. I let him have the painting three or four years after the accident because Carlo's mother wouldn't leave me alone about it.

Doctor (*to Di Nolli*) Your mother being his sister?

Di Nolli Yes. We're here because we promised her. She died a month ago. But for that, Frida and I would be on our honeymoon.

Doctor With your mind on other things – I understand.

Di Nolli Mother died convinced that her brother was about to get better.

Doctor And can you tell me why she thought so?

Di Nolli It was a conversation they had not long before she died.

Doctor Did they now? It would be useful to know what he said.

Di Nolli I wish I could help you. All I know, is she came back obviously upset. I gathered he'd spoken to her with unusual tenderness, almost as if he knew it was the last time . . . and on her deathbed she made me promise not to abandon him, to have him seen . . .

Doctor And here we are. So first, let's see . . . sometimes the tiniest event can . . . This portrait, then . . .

Matilda Oh, heavens, we mustn't exaggerate its importance – it was just that I hadn't seen it for so long.

Doctor Please . . . patience . . .

Di Nolli Well, quite – it's been hanging there for about fifteen years.

Matilda Nearer eighteen.

Doctor Please! – you don't know yet what I'm asking. In my belief these two portraits may be crucial. They were done, I suppose, before the famous – or should I say infamous – pageant, is that right?

Matilda Of course.

Doctor When he was still in his right mind – that's the point I was making. Were they his idea?

Matilda No, not at all. Lots of us who took part decided to have our portraits done as a souvenir of the pageant.

Belcredi I had mine done – Charles of Anjou.

Doctor You don't know if it was he who asked for it?

Matilda I've no idea. It's possible. Or it might have been Carlo's mother's idea of humouring him.

Doctor Now another thing. Was this pageant his idea?

Belcredi No, it was mine.

Matilda Don't take any notice of him. It was poor Belassi's idea.

Belcredi Belassi?

Matilda (*to the Doctor*) Count Belassi, poor man, who died two or three months later.

Belcredi But Belassi wasn't even there when I . . .

Di Nolli Excuse me, Doctor, does it really matter whose idea . . .

Doctor It could be important.

Belcredi It was mine! This is too much! Do you think I'd brag about it after what happened? You see, at the Club we'd been thinking of putting on a show for the next carnival. So I suggested this historical pageant – I say

15

historical, it was more of a hodge-podge, everyone had to choose a character from this or that century, a king, or emperor, or prince, with his lady – queen or empress, beside him, also on horseback. The horses had all the period trappings, too, of course. That was my suggestion and it was adopted.

Matilda Well, my invitation came from Belassi.

Belcredi Theft. He wasn't even in the Club that night. Nor was *he*.

Doctor So then he chose Henry?

Matilda That's because, my name being Matilda, I said off the top of my head that I'd be Countess Matilda of Tuscany. He said, in that case he'd be Henry IV.

Doctor I'm sorry, I don't see the connection.

Matilda I didn't either at first. He said he'd be at my feet just like at Canossa. I knew about Canossa but only vaguely, and when I looked it up I found I was the Pope's most zealous ally against the German Emperor. I went hot and cold. I understood why he'd chosen to be Henry IV.

Doctor You mean, perhaps, because . . .

Belcredi Dear God, Doctor – because he was mad about her, and she couldn't stand him.

Matilda That's not true! I didn't dislike him, quite the opposite. But whenever a man gets all serious about a woman –

Belcredi He turns into a complete ass . . .

Matilda No, he wasn't like you, my dear.

Belcredi But I've never asked to be taken seriously.

Matilda Don't we know it. But with him, you had to take him seriously back. (*to the Doctor*) Among the misfortunes we women have to put up with from time to time is suddenly being confronted by a pair of eyes gazing at us with the solemn promise of lifelong devotion. (*She bursts into laughter.*) There's nothing more ridiculous. If only men could see themselves doing their lifelong-devotion look. It always made me laugh. More so in those days. But now, after twenty years, let me confess something. When I laughed at him, it was partly out of fear, because, coming from him, you felt he could mean it. And that would have been extremely dangerous.

Doctor Now this, this is something I want to know about. Extremely dangerous, you say?

Matilda (*lightly*) Well, because he wasn't like the others . . . and I wasn't brave enough not to laugh it off . . . anyway, I had no patience with being serious. I was just a girl, I hadn't done my share of living, so I laughed along with the everyone else. I was sorry later . . . I hated myself, actually, because my laughing at him got all mixed up with those fools laughing at him.

Belcredi Like they do with me, more or less.

Matilda You make people laugh by humiliating yourself – that's the opposite.

Doctor So, as I understand it, he was already in a bit of a state.

Belcredi Yes, but in his own way.

Doctor What do you mean?

Belcredi Well, I'd say – dispassionately in a state.

Matilda What do you mean, dispassionately!? He threw himself into life –

Belcredi I'm not saying he was putting it on. Not at all. He was often worked up. But I'd swear he'd immediately dissociate himself from the state he was in, observing himself – even, in my view, when he was at his most spontaneous. I think, furthermore, it had a harmful effect on him. Sometimes he'd get into these hilarious fits of rage against himself.

Matilda That's true, he did.

Belcredi And why was that? (*to the Doctor*) The way I see it, that outside view of himself, like someone watching himself playing a part, separated him from what he was feeling – which then seemed to him not exactly fake, because he wasn't faking his feelings, but something he had to act out as a self-conscious intention, to make up for the authenticity he couldn't feel. So he would go to extremes, improvise, exaggerate, anything to lose his self-awareness . . . that's why he'd come across so erratic, frivolous, even at times ludicrous.

Doctor And . . . anti-social, would you say?

Belcredi No, not at all! He was game for anything – he was famous for organising dances, tableaux vivants, benefits – all for the fun of it, you see. But he was a very good actor, that's the point.

Di Nolli As a madman he's even more impressive, magnificent, terrifying.

Belcredi From the word go. Imagine it, when the accident happened and he was thrown . . .

Matilda It was dreadful. I was right next to him. I saw him under the hoofs, the horse bolting . . .

Belcredi At first we didn't think he was seriously hurt. There was some commotion, and the cavalcade came to a halt. People wanted to know what had happened, but he'd already been picked up and carried into the house.

Matilda There was nothing, not a scratch, no blood . . .

Belcredi We thought he'd just passed out.

Matilda Then, when a couple of hours later –

Belcredi Yes – he showed up in the hall, that's what I was coming to.

Matilda The look on his face – I noticed straight away.

Belcredi No you didn't, none of us did. We didn't realise, you see . . .

Matilda Well, of course *you* didn't – you were all acting like lunatics.

Belcredi We were acting our parts, having fun, it was a bear-garden.

Matilda You can imagine the shock when we realised he wasn't pretending.

Doctor Ah, you mean, because he . . .

Belcredi Yes, he joined in. We thought he'd recovered and was acting up like the rest of us – and better than us, because, as I said, he was very good. We thought he was playing along with everyone else.

Matilda They started flicking him with their whips . . .

Belcredi And then he drew his sword. He was armed as a king, of course. He started slashing his sword around at people . . . a terrifying moment for all of us.

Matilda I'll never forget it, those faces . . . distorted, appalled in the face of his fury, which was no longer a masquerade but madness unmasked –

Belcredi Henry IV himself, in a towering rage.

Matilda He'd been obsessed with the pageant for a month or more – it occupied him in everything he did. I'm sure that was part of the reason.

Belcredi And the way he did his homework! Every detail, no matter how trivial.

Doctor Well, it's classic. Fall from horse – hits head – brain damage – temporary obsession made permanent, fixed, causing a disturbance of the balance of the mind . . . up to insanity itself.

Belcredi (*to Frida and Di Nolli*) See what life has got up its sleeve, my darlings? (*to Di Nolli*) You must have been four or five. (*to Frida*) Your mother had her portrait done before she had any idea that one day she'd have a daughter who'd replace her in it. And I've gone grey. And he – (*pointing at the portrait*) – one bang on the head and time stops, he's Henry IV.

Doctor So, ladies and gentlemen, to sum up –

But Bertold enters, looking upset.

Bertold Sorry! . . . Sorry . . .

Frida (*panicked*) It's him!

Matilda Is it him?

Di Nolli No – it's all right . . .

Doctor Who is he?

Belcredi A leftover from the masquerade.

Di Nolli He's one of the young men we have here to keep him company.

Bertold I'm sorry, My Lord –

Di Nolli Sorry! I gave orders we were not to be disturbed!

Bertold Yes, sir, but I can't take any more, I want to give notice.

Di Nolli Oh, you're the one who was joining today.

Bertold Yes, sir, and what I'm telling you is, I've had enough.

Matilda So he's not as calm as you made out.

Bertold No, My Lady, it's not him, it's those other three – talk about him needing humouring, My Lord, they're the crazy ones round here –

> *Landolf and Harold enter in a hurry, anxious, but stopping at the threshold.*

Landolf Can we come in?

Harold Begging your pardon, sir . . .

Di Nolli Come in! – What's going on? What do you think you're doing?

Frida (*scared*) I'm going, I don't like this –

Di Nolli Don't, Frida . . .

Landolf My Lord, this fool . . .

Bertold Oh, thanks very much –

Harold He ruined everything, sir, by barging out of there –

Landolf Himself is now beside himself, we can't hold him, he's ordered his arrest and wants to pronounce sentence from the throne – what should we do?

Di Nolli Lock the door!

> *Landolf goes and locks the door.*

Harold Ordulf can't hold him on his own.

Landolf My Lord, maybe if we announce them right away, to distract him . . . If you gentlemen know who you . . .

Di Nolli Yes, it's all decided . . . (*to the Doctor*) If you're ready, Doctor . . .

Frida Well, I'm not, Carlo! I'm going – please come, Mother, please . . .

Doctor I say, he's not armed, is he?

Di Nolli Of course not! Frida, don't be a baby – you wanted to come.

Frida No I didn't, it was Mummy.

Matilda Well, I'm ready. What do we have to do?

Belcredi Is it really necessary for me to dress up?

Landolf Absolutely essential, sir! Look at us. I'm afraid there'll be hell to pay if he saw you dressed like that.

Harold He'd think it's the work of the devil.

Landolf What's worse he might think it's the work of his deadly enemy.

Belcredi Gregory VII!

Landolf Exactly. He calls him the Anti-Christ.

Belcredi The Pope? – That's a good one.

Landolf Yes, sir – and says he brings the dead to life, practises all the diabolical arts – he's terrified of him.

Doctor Paranoia, quite normal.

Harold He'd lose control.

Di Nolli (*to Belcredi*) We can wait outside – it's only the Doctor who has to see him.

Doctor What, you mean on my own?

Di Nolli They'll be with you!

Doctor Ah, no, I thought the Countess . . .

Matilda I do – I am – I'm staying – of course I'm staying, I want to see him again!

Frida What for, Mummy? – Please come . . .

Matilda (*imperiously*) Stop it – this is what I came for. (*to Landolf*) I'll be . . . the mother-in-law, Adelaide.

Landolf Right. Bertha's mother, fine, you won't need any more than a cloak and a coronet . . . (*to Harold*) Get on with it, Harry.

Harold What about the Doctor?

Doctor Yes . . . we thought, the Bishop . . . Bishop Hugo of Cluny.

Harold Abbot of Cluny, sir – right . . .

Landolf He's been here lots of times.

Doctor Lots of . . . ?

Landolf No problem, it's a simple costume.

Doctor But . . .

Landolf He won't remember you, he doesn't take in faces, only the clothes.

Matilda That should help.

Di Nolli We'll go, Frida – come on, Tito.

Belcredi If she's staying, I'm staying.

Matilda I don't need you here.

Belcredi I didn't say you needed me – I'd like to see him again, too, any objections?

Landolf It might look better if there were three of you.

Harold So, what's he . . .?

Belcredi Oh, just find something simple for me . . .

Landolf (*to Harold*) A Clunatic.

Belcredi A Clunatic? What's that?

Landolf The Abbot of Cluny's retinue – in a Benedictine habit. (*to Harold*) Go, go! (*to Bertold*) You, too – and keep out of sight for the rest of the day. No – wait – (*to Bertold*) bring in the costumes he gives you. (*to Harold*) And then go and announce they're coming – Duchess Adelaide and Monsignor Hugo of Cluny, got it?

Harold and Bertold exit.

Di Nolli We'll make ourselves scarce.

Di Nolli and Frida exit.

Doctor (*to Landolf*) He likes me, doesn't he? – I mean, Hugo of Cluny?

Landolf Yes, don't worry, Monsignor has always been received with the greatest respect here. You don't worry yourself either, My Lady. He never forgets that you both spoke up for him when he'd been waiting two days in the snow, half-frozen outside Canossa and the Pope let him in finally . . .

Belcredi And what about me?

Landolf You just keep back and act respectful.

Matilda I wish you'd wait outside.

Belcredi Aren't you getting a bit . . .?

Matilda Whatever I'm getting, I'm getting. Leave me alone.

Bertold returns with the garments.

Landolf Ah – wardrobe! The cloak for the Countess.

Matilda Wait, I'll take off my hat.

Landolf (*to Bertold*) Lose the hat. (*to Matilda*) May I?

Matilda Aren't there any mirrors here?

Landolf Outside. If your ladyship would rather see to herself . . .?

Matilda That would be better, let me have it, I'll be back in a minute.

Matilda takes her hat and goes out with Bertold, who is carrying her cloak and coronet. Meanwhile the Doctor and Belcredi put on the Benedictine robes as best they can.

Belcredi I wasn't frankly expecting to join the Benedictines. It's a pretty expensive form of insanity, this!

Doctor None of them come cheap.

Belcredi Yes, but when there's a fortune at one's disposal . . .

Landolf You're right, sir – we have an entire costume department, everything perfectly made from period patterns. It's my personal responsibility to commission trained costumiers. We spend a mint.

Matilda re-enters wearing cloak and coronet.

Belcredi Ah! – beautiful! You look like a queen.

Matilda You look like an ostrich in Holy Orders. Take it off.

Belcredi Have you seen the Doctor?

Doctor I know, it's too bad . . . never mind . . .

Matilda No, the Doctor's fine . . . but you, you are ridiculous!

Doctor (*to Landolf*) Does he receive people often?

Landolf It depends. Sometimes he demands to see this or that character, and then we have to find somebody who's willing . . . Women, too.

Matilda Oh? – Women, too?

Belcredi You don't say. In costume? (*pointing at Matilda*) Like that?

Landolf Well, you know, women who'll do it.

Belcredi Ah. (*to Matilda*) Watch yourself – this could be tricky.

Harold enters, gesturing for silence.

Harold His Majesty the Emperor!

Ordulf and Harold take their positions. Ordulf holds the imperial crown, Harold the sceptre with the eagle and the orb with the cross. Henry IV enters.

Henry (*bowing*) My Lady . . . Monsignor . . . (*Henry sees Belcredi, and is about to bow to him too, but turns to Landolf, and whispers.*) Isn't that Peter Damian?

Landolf No, Your Majesty, he's a monk from Cluny attending the Abbot.

Henry Peter Damian! It's no good looking to the Duchess, Peter! On my oath, Duchess, I've had a change

26

of heart towards your daughter. I admit I wanted to divorce her and would have done if he hadn't stopped me – because there were others who'd have played along – the Bishop of Mainz for one, he was willing for a hundred and twenty farms . . . (*He glances at Landolf, a little lost, and quickly says:*) Still, I shouldn't be speaking ill of clerics here . . . (*becoming humble again with Belcredi*) I'm grateful now, believe me, I'm grateful to you for stopping me. My life has been one humiliation after another . . . and now here I am in sackcloth as you see. (*suddenly changing tone*) Bear up. Clear head, shoulders back – (*resuming*) I know how to correct my path where I have erred – I'll even prostrate myself before you, Peter Damian. I take it it's not you who's been putting it about that my saintly mother spread her legs for the Bishop of Augsburg?

Belcredi Er, no, that wasn't me.

Henry Ha! The nerve of it. (*staring at Belcredi*) No, I don't think you've got it in you. (*tugging the Doctor's sleeve*) It's always 'them', isn't that so, Monsignor?

Harold (*quietly prompting the Doctor*) Oh yes, those grasping bishops . . .

Doctor Right, yes . . . them . . .

Henry They'd stop at nothing. Poor little boy that I was, playing with my toys, a king and didn't know it . . . I was six when they tore me away from my mother, an innocent to be used against her, against the dynasty itself . . . profaning, picking and stealing . . .

Landolf Your Majesty . . .

Henry Yes, all right. But these disgraceful slanders against my mother are going too far. I cannot even mourn her, Duchess. I turn to you because you must have a mother's heart. She came to see me, from her convent, a month ago. They tell me she's dead. (*smiling sadly*) But I can't grieve for her, because if you're here and I'm in sackcloth, that means I'm twenty-six.

Harold (*whispering, comforting*) So it follows she can't be dead, Your Majesty.

Henry So I'll grieve for her all in good time. (*Henry shows Matilda his hair colour, almost coquettishly.*) Look! – Still blond! (*confidentially*) For you. I don't care for myself. Though it helps . . . a little touch . . . trim the sails of time, you follow me, Monsignor? (*Henry goes to look at her hair.*) Oh, I see that you, too . . . Italians! Tsk! Far be it from me to criticise . . . Nobody likes to acknowledge the mortality that sets limits to our will. But we're born and we die, that's what I say! Did you want to be born, Monsignor? I didn't. And between birth and death, neither of our choosing, many things happen we wouldn't have chosen, which reluctantly – we have to accept.

Doctor (*studying Henry closely*) True . . . sad but true.

Henry You see, when we refuse to resign ourselves, what's the result? Wishful thinking at its most futile. A woman who wishes she were a man . . . an old man who wishes he were young . . . None of us lies or pretends – what happens is, in all sincerity, we inhabit the self we have chosen for ourselves, and don't let go. But while you're holding tight, gripping on to your monk's robe, Monsignor, from out your sleeve something slips away without you noticing: your life! And how surprised you'll be when you suddenly see it going, gone – how you'll despise yourself – and how sorry you'll be, oh yes, if you only knew how often I've grieved over mine, slithering off – it had my face, but so disfigured I had to turn away. (*Henry approaches Matilda.*) Has that never happened to you, My Lady? Do you think of yourself unchanging and unchanged? Oh God, but there was a day . . . How could you? How could you have done that? (*He stares into Matilda's eyes.*) Yes – that. We understand each other. Don't worry, it's our secret. And you, Peter Damian . . . that you could be friends with someone like that!

Landolf Your Majesty . . .

Henry No names. I know how upset people get. (*Henry turns to Belcredi.*) Do you agree? We all hug our idea of ourselves to ourselves. As our hair turns greyer, we keep pace with the colouring bottle. It's of no consequence that I fool nobody. You, Duchess, don't fool yourself or anybody else – perhaps the image in your mirror, just a tiny bit. I do it to amuse myself. You do it in earnest. But no amount of earnestness stops it being a masquerade, and I'm not referring to your cloak and coronet. I'm talking about a memory of yourself you want to hold tight, the memory of a day gone by when to be fair-haired was your delight – or dark-haired if you were dark: the faded memory of being young. With you, it's different, Peter Damian. The memory of who you were, what you did, is no more than a dream that's safe with you – isn't that so? – a bad dream. It's the same for me. Dreams, many of them, now I think of it, with no meaning I can explain. Oh, well! – Nothing to be done, and tomorrow will be more of the same. (*Henry flies into a sudden fury, grabbing the sackcloth he's wearing.*) This sackcloth . . .!

> *Then, with a wild joy, Henry makes as if to rip the sackcloth off, while Harold and Ordulf, frightened, rush to stop him.*

Damn and blast it! (*backing away, shouting, taking off his sackcloth*) Tomorrow in Brixen, twenty-seven bishops from Germany and Lombardy will sign my petition for the removal of that impostor Gregory VII!

Ordulf Your Majesty, please, for God's sake . . .

Harold (*urging him with signs to put his sackcloth back on*) Don't say that, Your Majesty . . . The Abbot's here with the Duchess to intercede on your behalf.

Surreptitiously Harold makes signs to the Doctor, urging him to say something quickly.

Doctor (*confused*) Ah – yes – that's it – we're here to intercede . . .

Henry allows the three counsellors to put the sackcloth back on his shoulders.

Henry Yes – forgive me – forgive me . . . Monsignor . . . My Lady . . . God be my witness, it's the burden of excommunication lying on me like a dead weight . . . (*quietly to Landolf, Harold and Ordulf*) I don't know what it is, but I just can't bring myself to grovel to that man.

Landolf That's because, Your Majesty, you've convinced yourself he's Peter Damian when he isn't!

Henry He isn't?

Harold No, he's just some poor monk, Your Majesty.

Henry None of us is the best judge of our actions when we act on instinct. Perhaps it takes a woman to understand me. Think of your daughter, Duchess – think of Bertha – I told you how my heart has changed.

Henry suddenly turns to Belcredi and shouts in his face, as if he had denied it.

30

Changed – changed – by the love and devotion she has shown me at this terrible time!

Henry stops, shaken by his own outburst of fury, and tries to contain himself, with a cry of exasperation in his throat; then he turns back to Matilda, in gentle and sorrowful humility.

She's come with me, My Lady, she's waiting in the courtyard. She chose to follow me like a beggar, and she's frozen from two nights out in the snow! You're her mother, doesn't it stir you to pity? – to go with him – (*He points at the Doctor.*) – and implore the Pope to receive me and grant forgiveness?

Matilda (*shaking*) Oh, yes . . . yes . . . and at once . . .

Doctor We'll do it! We'll do it!

Henry And another thing! One more thing! (*Henry calls them all round him and whispers in great secret.*) Receiving me is not enough. You know he can do . . . anything. Even raise the dead. (*beating his chest*) Well, here I am. As you see me. There's no magic he can't overcome. My real punishment is this – (*Henry points at his picture on the wall, almost fearful.*) – that! – Look at it – to be hostage to that apparition! I'm a penitent now and a penitent I'll remain, I swear to God, until His Holiness receives me. But once the anathema has been lifted, please, both of you, beg the Pope to do this one thing, because he can do it: set me free from that, there, so that – wretched as it is – I can live my own life. (*pointing at the picture on the wall*) You can't stay twenty-six for ever! I'm asking this for Bertha, too – so I can love her as she deserves to be loved.

There. That's it. I am in your hands. (*bowing*) My Lady! Monsignor!

Henry heads back, still bowing, but then he notices Belcredi, who has come closer to listen: he fears he may want to steal the imperial crown, which is sitting on the throne. Henry rushes to pick it up and hide it under his sackcloth. Then, with a sly smile he bows repeatedly and exits. Matilda is so shocked she collapses into a chair, almost fainting.

Act Two

Another room in the villa, adjoining the throne room, furnished in a plain antique style. Late afternoon of the same day. Onstage are Matilda, the Doctor and Belcredi. Matilda is keeping apart, preoccupied and on edge.

Belcredi Well . . . pretty straightforward so far, wouldn't you say? . . . He wasn't fooled. He told us himself in so many words. (*to Matilda*) You heard him, didn't you?

Matilda What . . .? Yes, but it wasn't what you think.

Doctor He was talking about our robes . . . your cloak . . . He responded to our costumes the way a child would.

Matilda A child? What are you talking about?

Doctor On one level. On another it's more complicated than you can imagine.

Matilda Not to me – it was plain as day.

Doctor To you, perhaps, but we must bear in mind the peculiar psychology of the mad – they can see right through any disguise, while at the same time suspending their disbelief, like children at play believing in their make-believe. That's why I say he is in one sense like a child while in another it's complicated – because, you see, *his* make-believe – and he is well aware of it – is that he is the image of that image in the picture frame.

Belcredi He did say that.

Doctor There you are. Then what happens? – His image is joined by other images: us, do you follow me? And

33

with that shrewd insight of the madman, he immediately spotted the difference between us and him, he spotted the pretence; which made him suspicious. But he kept his suspicions to himself. That's what madmen do. And that's all there is to it! Of course, he didn't see that we were doing it all for his sake. What made the game all the more pitiful is that he kept trying – in his coy, obstinate way – to tell us it was only a game – *his* game – hence the make-up and how he only puts it on for fun, and so on.

Matilda No, you haven't got it.

Doctor What do you . . .?

Matilda The plain fact is he recognised me.

Doctor That's impossible.

Belcredi (*at the same time*) He couldn't have.

Matilda I'm telling you he recognised me. When he looked into my eyes, he knew me.

Belcredi But he was talking to you about Bertha, your daughter.

Matilda He was talking about me – me!

Belcredi Well, yes, he did mention –

Matilda My dyed hair, exactly – and how quickly he added – didn't you notice? – 'or dark-haired if you were dark'. He remembered perfectly well that back then my hair was dark.

Belcredi No, no . . .

Matilda (*to the Doctor*) My hair is naturally dark, like Frida's. That's what got him talking about my daughter.

Belcredi What daughter? He's never seen your daughter.

Matilda That's my point, you idiot – everything he said about my pretend daughter *now*, he was saying about me *then*!

Belcredi It's catching!

Matilda Oh, don't be so stupid.

Belcredi Excuse me, but when were you ever his wife? He's got a wife – in his mad mind she's Bertha of Susa and you're her mother.

Matilda I'm not denying I came to him as Duchess Adelaide – being blonde and not dark any more, the way he remembered me, I decided to be his mother-in-law. But the daughter doesn't exist for him, he's never seen her, he doesn't even know I've got a daughter – so how could he know what colour her hair is?

Belcredi He didn't say he knew. He was just speaking generally . . . Good God, he was only making a point about people colouring their hair to look younger than they are – blondes, brunettes . . . and as usual you go off at a tangent.

Matilda No . . . no . . . I don't care what you say, he was talking to me about me, everything he said . . .

Belcredi I couldn't get a word in edgeways, and it was all about you! What? – even when he was talking to Peter Damian?

Matilda Indirectly, yes. Or perhaps you have another explanation why he took an instant dislike to you?

Doctor (*after an awkward pause*) Well, perhaps it was simply that it was only Duchess Adelaide and the Abbot of Cluny who were announced . . . and seeing there was a third person there made him mistrustful.

Belcredi There you are. His mistrust made him leery of me, and she has to insist it was because he recognised her.

Matilda Well, he did! You know that look where you just *know*. It was just a flash . . . I don't know how to put it . . .

Doctor A moment of lucidity . . .

Matilda Yes! And from then on everything he said seemed to be steeped in regret, for his youth, and mine, because of the awful thing that happened to him, that froze him in that mask he longs to be free of.

Belcredi Oh, yes! – Free to love your daughter, as he said – or, in your version, to love you – touched by your compassion perhaps?

Matilda And compassion is very much what I'm feeling, believe me.

Belcredi Oh, I do! – It's like a miracle.

Doctor May I speak? I don't deal in miracles, we doctors aren't medicine men. I listened very carefully to everything he said, and, as I would put it, there's a relaxation in the coherence which is typical of systematised delusion; it's clearly – how can I put it – relaxed; the coherence of the delusion isn't, er, cohering as before. He can't quite find the point of equilibrium between ego and super-ego . . . A sudden memory deflects him, not – and this is very encouraging – not into incipient inertia but rather into a melancholic reflex, which indicates . . . yes, significant cerebral activity. As I say, very encouraging. Now, with the shock tactic we have decided on –

Matilda Why isn't the car back? It's over three hours . . .

Doctor What?

36

Matilda The car! It's been over three hours!

Doctor (*looking at his watch*) Four, actually.

Matilda It should have been back ages ago. But as usual . . .

Doctor Maybe they can't find the dress.

Matilda I told them exactly where it was. And where's Frida?

Belcredi In the garden with Carlo.

Doctor Getting her over her nervousness . . .

Belcredi It wasn't nerves, it was a tantrum.

Matilda Don't try to force her, believe me, I know her.

Doctor Let's not rush things. We have to wait till it's dark, and it won't take a minute to set up. If we can give him a shock and snap the thread which binds him to his delusion, give him back what he longs for – he said it himself: you can't stay twenty-six for ever! – and free him from his prison – that's the way he sees it –

Belcredi – he'll be cured! Saved by the alienation technique!

Doctor His clock stopped, and we're checking our watches for the critical moment when . . . with a quick shake, we might get his clock ticking again, after all this time.

Di Nolli enters.

Matilda Carlo! Where's Frida?

Di Nolli She's coming.

Doctor Is the car back?

Di Nolli Yes.

Matilda It is? With the dress?

Di Nolli It's been back a while.

Doctor Excellent!

Matilda Well, where is she? And the dress . . . ?

Di Nolli You'll see in a moment. Here she comes.

Bertold (*entering*) Her Highness the Countess of Canossa!

Frida enters, the image of the portrait.

Frida Of Tuscany, if you don't mind. Canossa is just one of my castles.

Belcredi Just look at her! Look at her! She's a different person.

Matilda She's me! My God, can you see? Stop there, Frida! She's my portrait come to life!

Doctor Yes . . . Perfect!

Belcredi It's amazing.

Frida Don't anybody make me laugh or I'll burst. Was your waist really so tiny, Mummy? I'm having to hold my stomach in.

Matilda Wait . . . Hold still . . . These creases, is it that tight on you?

Frida I can barely breathe. You better make it quick . . .

Doctor But we have to wait till dark . . .

Frida I can't hold myself in till dark!

Matilda Why did you put it on so early?

Frida I couldn't resist. The minute I saw it . . .

Doctor Would you stand over there . . . here . . . not quite so close . . . now forward just a little . . .

Belcredi For the full effect of twenty years between.

Matilda What a disaster, eh?

Belcredi Oh, I wouldn't go so far as that.

Doctor No, not at all! I only meant the dress . . . I meant . . . to compare . . .

Belcredi As for the dress, it's not twenty years, more like a thousand. That's some shake for anybody's clock. (*pointing first at Frida and then at Matilda*) From there to there? You'll have to pick him up with a spoon. Think about it. Seriously: for us it's twenty years, two dresses, a masquerade . . . but if time stopped for him nearly a thousand years ago . . . Oh, you don't think so?

Doctor No. Because life doesn't stop. When the illusion is stripped away, you've caught up – the jump is not a thousand years, it's only twenty.

Belcredi I've had a thought. Look at Frida and her mother. Who's ahead of whom? The older generation, that's who. The young think they're leading the way but they've got it backwards. We're years ahead of them, because we've been at it longer.

Doctor Ah, if only time didn't come between us like a wedge!

Belcredi It doesn't. Young people still have to go through what we went through . . . get older, make more or less the same mistakes. It's an illusion that you leave life by a door ahead of the one you entered by. You're dying the moment you're born . . . those who started first are beating the path for those who follow. Look at her! (*He points at Frida.*) Centuries ahead of us, the Countess Matilda of Tuscany.

Di Nolli Please. Tito – stop fooling.

Belcredi Oh, you think I'm fooling?

Di Nolli Ever since you got here.

Belcredi Me? I even dressed up as a monk for you. I promise you, Doctor, I still don't understand what you're up to.

Doctor You will. Mind you, not with the Countess still dressed like that . . .

Belcredi Ah – you mean she, too . . . will have to . . .

Doctor Of course! Wearing a similar dress which we've got ready for her, so he thinks she's the Countess Matilda of Canossa, too.

Frida Tuscany, Tuscany!

Belcredi Oh . . . I see. He'll be confronted by two . . .

Doctor Exactly. Two of them. And then . . .

Frida (*with Di Nolli*) Doctor – can you come here a minute and explain something . . . ?

Doctor Of course . . .

Belcredi (*to Matilda*) My God . . . So then . . .

Matilda Then what?

Belcredi Does he mean so much to you? To lend yourself to this farrago? It's quite something for a woman to . . .

Matilda For most women, perhaps.

Belcredi Oh no, my dear, for any woman! To demean herself . . .

Matilda I feel responsible.

Belcredi No you don't. You know you'd never suffer the indignity.

Matilda So if I wouldn't, what are you talking about? Where's the indignity?

Belcredi Oh, not so as *they'd* catch on, just enough to humiliate me.

Matilda As if anyone's thinking of you at this moment!

Di Nolli Right – we're all set . . . (*to Bertold*) You – get one of those three in here.

Bertold (*leaving*) Right away.

Matilda But first we have to pretend we're leaving.

Di Nolli Quite so – that's why I've called him to announce your departure. (*to Belcredi*) There's no need for you to be there.

Belcredi Naturally . . . no need for me . . . no need at all . . .

Di Nolli And anyway, you might arouse his suspicion again, you see?

Belcredi I do see. A bit part.

Landolf, followed by Bertold, enters from the door on the right.

Landolf Excuse me . . .

Di Nolli Come in, come in . . . You're Lolo, aren't you?

Landolf Lolo or Landolpho, My Lord, I answer to both.

Di Nolli Good. Now, the Doctor and the Countess will take their leave . . .

Landolf No problem. We'll tell him the Pope's agreed to receive them. Himself's in his quarters, sorry for everything he said and worrying His Holiness won't give him absolution. If you'd be so good, now put the costumes back on . . .

Doctor Yes – right – let's get on with it.

Landolf One other thing, if I may suggest. Tell him the Countess Matilda of Tuscany is all for it, begging the Pope on Himself's behalf.

Matilda You see? He did recognise me!

Landolf No. Excuse me. It's only that with His Holiness being under the Countess's roof, Himself is frightened it'll count against him. It's a funny thing – you'll know better than me – but so far as I can see there's nothing in the history books about Henry IV being secretly in love with Matilda of Tuscany.

Matilda No, there isn't. On the contrary.

Landolf That's what I thought. But he's always saying how he loved you, and now he's terrified you hating him might do for him with the Pope.

Belcredi Well, we must find a way to convince him that this aversion of hers is a thing of the past!

Landolf Fine. I'll tell him that.

Matilda Yes, why don't you? (*to Belcredi*) Because, in case you didn't know, my dear, history records precisely that – the Pope yielded to the entreaties of Matilda and the Abbot of Cluny . . . and if you want to know, at the time, during the pageant, my intention was to remind him . . . to show him my feelings were not as unfriendly as he imagined.

Belcredi Well, how wonderful . . . to have history on your side.

Landolf Well, if that's the case, why dress up twice over? – You could go in with the Monsignor dressed as the Countess of Tuscany.

Doctor No! – for God's sake! That would ruin everything! He's got to see the two of them together. No, listen, My Lady, you're still the mother-in-law, Adelaide. We leave. He sees us go. That's vital. Come along, there's no time to lose.

Landolf, Matilda and the Doctor leave.

Frida I'm starting to feel nervous.

Di Nolli Not again?

Frida It wouldn't be so bad if I'd seen him earlier.

Di Nolli There's nothing to be afraid of.

Frida He's not going to be violent?

Di Nolli No – he's perfectly calm.

Belcredi Melancholic. Haven't you heard he's secretly in love with you?

Frida That's what worries me.

Belcredi He won't hurt you.

Di Nolli It'll be over before you know it.

Frida Yes, but alone with him, and it'll be dark . . .

Di Nolli I'll be close by – and the others will be behind the door waiting, ready to rush in. As soon as he sees your mother, your part's over.

Belcredi What *I'm* afraid of, on the other hand, is that it'll all be for nothing.

Di Nolli Oh, don't you start! I have every faith in this cure.

Frida So have I. I'm getting quite excited.

Belcredi But you see, darlings, what we're forgetting is that madmen, though sadly they don't know it, bless them . . . don't think rationally!

Di Nolli What's that got to do with anything?

Belcredi What! – when he sees her (*pointing at Frida*) and then her mother, aren't we counting on him to apply his reason? – We've orchestrated the whole thing just for that.

Di Nolli What do you mean, reason? The doctor's just confronting him with his own make-believe doubled up, that's all.

Belcredi For the life of me I can never understand why these people are allowed to call themselves doctors.

Di Nolli What people?

Belcredi Psychiatrists. Why do they graduate in *medicine*?

Di Nolli What else should they graduate in?

Belcredi Rhetoric . . . It's only about who has the best lines . . . 'coherence typical of systematised delusion' . . . 'melancholic reflex' . . . The first thing they tell you is they don't perform miracles when a miracle is exactly what's needed – they know that's how to be taken seriously . . . and the miracle is they get away with it.

Bertold (*peeping*) They're coming! Coming this way!

Di Nolli Are you sure?

Bertold It looks like he's seeing them out! Yes . . . here he comes!

Di Nolli Let's get out of here. You stay.

Bertold Me?

*Di Nolli, Frida and Belcredi hurry out, leaving
Bertold behind, confused and lost. Landolf enters
bowing, followed by Matilda, with cloak and coronet,
as in Act One, and the Doctor, in the robes of the
Abbot of Cluny. Henry IV is between them, in regal
attire, followed by Ordulf and Harold.*

Henry I'm asking you: do you think I'm mulish or foxy?
(*Pause.*) A mule, then.

Doctor A mule? Heaven forbid that I . . .

Henry So you think I'm really a fox?

Doctor No, not a mule and not a fox either.

Henry Come, Abbot, since one can't be both I was
hoping that in denying me the obstinacy of the one you'd
grant me the cleverness of the other. I assure you I could
do with a little of it. But I suppose you reserve it all for
yourself.

Doctor Who, me? Do I seem clever to you?

Henry No, Monsignor! What an idea! (*addressing
Matilda*) Could you spare me a moment before you go?
(*anxiously, in private*) Do you truly love your daughter?

Matilda Yes, of course I do . . .

Henry So, do you wish me to love and cherish her to
make up for all the wrongs I've done her? . . . Not that
you should credit the debauchery my enemies accuse
me of.

Matilda I don't. I never did.

Henry Well, then, is that what you'd have me do?

Matilda What?

45

Henry Fall in love with your daughter again? (*Pauses, looks at her intently.*) Watch out for the Countess of Tuscany – she's not to be trusted.

Matilda But – as I told you – she's begged and beseeched His Holiness no less than we have . . .

Henry Don't say that! Don't! Can't you see what it does to me?

Matilda looks at him and speaks to him quietly, sharing a confidence.

Matilda Do you still love her?

Henry Still? What do you mean, still? Nobody knows about that – nobody must know it.

Matilda But perhaps she knows . . . and that's why she went on her knees to the Pope for you . . .

Henry And you say you love your daughter! (*Pause, lightly.*) Well, Monsignor! It's all too true, about me finding out too late – far too late – that I had a wife . . . and still have her, there's no doubt about that . . . and I swear I never give her a thought. It may be a sin, but I feel nothing for her. What's astonishing, though, is neither does her mother! Admit it, Duchess, you don't give a damn about her. (*agitated*) She keeps on about that other woman! She goes on and on about her, I can't think why.

Landolf Perhaps, Your Majesty, it's because she thinks you've got the wrong idea about the Countess of Tuscany. (*embarrassed*) I mean the wrong idea just at the present time.

Henry Why, do you think I can trust her, too?

Landolf At this moment I do, Your Majesty.

Matilda You see? And that's why . . .

Henry Yes, I see. So, it's not that you think I love her. I see. I see. Nobody has ever thought so. So much the better. So that's enough about that. (*Henry stops. He turns to the Doctor with a completely different mood and expression.*) Monsignor, did you notice this? – The conditions the Pope has made for the revoking of my excommunication have absolutely nothing to do with the reason he excommunicated me in the first place. Tell Pope Gregory we'll meet in Brixen. And you, My Lady, if you happen to see your daughter in the castle courtyard of your friend the Countess . . . what can I say? Tell her she can come up here. We'll see whether she's the one who'll stay by me as wife and Empress. I've had lots of them coming here assuring me that they were her . . . though they knew I'd already . . . and sometimes I'd . . . well, why not? – it's my wife! But they all . . . when they'd tell me they were Bertha, and from Susa . . . I don't know why, they'd all start giggling. (*confidentially*) You know what I mean – in bed – not dressed up like this – the woman, too, naked . . . stripped down to male and female as nature made us, we forget who we are. Our clothes hanging up, watching over us like ghosts . . . (*to the Doctor*) What I think, Monsignor, is that ghosts for the most part are fragments of the unconscious escaping from our dreams, which when we sometimes see them wide-awake, in broad daylight, startle us. I'm always frightened in the night when they appear – all those disjointed images, people laughing, riders got down from their horses . . . I'm frightened sometimes by the blood pounding through my veins in the stillness of the night, like the heavy thud of footsteps in distant rooms . . . But I've kept you standing here long enough. My respects, Duchess, and regards to you, Monsignor.

Matilda and the Doctor bow in return, and leave. Henry closes the door and turns around, changed.

What a bunch of wankers! I played them like a kiddy-piano with a different colour for every key – it only needed the merest touch . . . white, red, yellow, green . . . and that other one, Peter Damian! – Ha! I saw through him all right! He didn't dare show his face again!

Henry, in an exuberant frenzy, suddenly sees Bertold, who is both stunned and frightened. Henry stops in front of him, pointing out Bertold to his three companions, and shakes him by the shoulders.

Look at this idiot here, with his mouth open! Do you understand now? – how I got them dressed up to perform for me? – those clowns wetting their pants in terror . . . in case I whip off their masks! – as if it wasn't me who made them dress up for my own entertainment while I play the madman!

Landolf, Harold *and* **Ordulf** (*overlapping*) Eh? – What? – What's he –?

Henry Well, I'm sick of this joke! Enough! You're all getting on my tits! My God, the nerve of that woman! – showing up here with her lover! With that air of stooping to this charade out of the goodness of their hearts! – so as not to make even madder a poor wretch already shut off from the world, from life! Well, who else would put up with that kind of persecution? These are people who every living moment expect everyone else to be how they see them! – Oh, but this can't be persecution! – not at all! – it's only their mode of thinking, living, feeling – each to his own! And you to yours, right? Of course! But what is yours? To be sheep! – feeble, flock-driven . . . and they make the most of that, they have you seeing and thinking and feeling the same as them. Or so they like to think. Because, when all's said and done, what do they do it with? Words, words, words. Simple words, which anyone can make mean whatever they like. That's what's called public opinion! God help anyone who finds the public's got a word for him . . . 'crazy', or, I don't know, 'imbecile'? Tell me something. Would you be so calm if you knew that there are people out there determined to make the world see you the way they want you to be seen? – to force their view of you and their valuation of you on everyone else? 'Loony!' 'Crackpot!' Don't imagine I'm doing all this as a madman now. Before I hit my head falling off a horse . . . (*Henry suddenly stops, noticing the four young men are agitated, dismayed and confused.*) What are you staring at each other for? Trying to decide? Is he or isn't he? All right, then, I'm a loony! Well, by God, on your knees, then! Kneel! I command you to get on your knees and touch the ground with your foreheads, three times. Get down! That's what you do when you're confronted by a maniac! (*Jeers.*) Oh, get up, for God's sake! Sheep! Why didn't you put me in a straitjacket? You're crushed by the weight of a word that weighs less than a fly. Our whole lives, crushed by the weight of words, empty words. Here I am. Do you really think Henry IV is alive? Yet, you're alive – and you let me order you about. I've got you where I want you. Do you think it's funny, that a dead man won't lie down? Well, maybe it's a joke in here, but go outside, into the world that's actually alive. The day breaks – it's dawn, the day's ahead of us, you say, it's ours to make. Really? You really think so? Goodbye to the beaten track – off with your hand-me-downs! Start talking. Repeat all the words that have ever been said. Do you think you're living now? Well, you're not. You're chewing on dead men's cud. (*stopping in front of Bertold, who is now completely dazed*) You haven't understood a thing, have you? What's your name?

Bertold My name . . . er, Bertold.

Henry Bertold, my arse. Just between you and me, what's your name?

Bertold Well, actually, it's Fino.

Henry Fino what?

Bertold Fino Pagliuca, sir.

Henry I've often heard you using your names. You're Lolo?

Landolf Yes, sir. (*joyfully*) Oh, my God, you mean . . .?

Henry (*sharply*) I mean what?

Landolf No . . . I only . . .

Henry Aren't I crazy any more? No, of course not, let's have a good laugh at those who think I am. (*to Harold*) You're Franco . . . (*to Ordulf*) And you, let me think . . .

Ordolfo Momo!

Henry That's it! Momo! Nice name.

Landolf But then . . . Oh, God . . .

Henry What? Nothing, let's have a good laugh about it, just the five of us. Ha, ha, ha, ha, ha!

Landolf, Harold and Ordulf are unsure, confused, glad and bewildered at the same time. They are whispering together.

Stop that whispering! (*to Bertold*) You're not laughing? Did I offend you? I wasn't talking about you, you know. It's everyone. It suits them to make out that someone is crazy so they can shut him away. Do you know why? Because they can't bear to hear what he might say . . . what I might say about those three who just left. I might say one's a slut, one's a dirty lecher and the third's a quack. Surely not! – who'd believe such a thing! Yet they'd all be listening horrified. But why? If it's not true? That's what I'd like to know. You shouldn't believe a madman. But they listen, wide-eyed with horror. Explain. Go on – I'm quite calm, as you see.

Bertold Maybe . . . it's because they think . . .

Henry No, no, look at me! I'm not saying it's true – nothing is true – but look into my eyes.

Bertold I am.

Henry What do you see? Yourself. See? See the fear in your eyes? Because now you think I'm mad. I've proved my point.

Landolf What point?

Henry You're alarmed because you think I'm still crazy. Well, why wouldn't you, for heaven's sake? You've believed it all this time, haven't you? Well, have you or haven't you? (*He sees they are terrified.*) Feel it now? – the ground disappearing under your feet, the air knocked out of your body? What do you expect? – faced with a madman? – with someone who shakes the foundations of everything you've shored up, inside and out? – Your logic! Right? Of course! Madmen, lucky them, don't build logically. Or with the logic of a feather on the breeze, this way, that way, day to day. You hold everything tight; madmen let everything go. You say: this can't be; they say: everything can be! But now you're thinking: not true. Because it's not true for you – and you – and you – and to a hundred thousand others. All right, let's look at what they think is the truth, the sane majority – what a show they make with their common ground, their wonderful logic. When I was a child the moon in the bottom of a well was real to me. And many other things, too. I believed everything I was told and I was happy. Heaven help you if you don't cling to your own reality,

51

even if yesterday's is contradicted by tomorrow's. Pray God you don't find out the thing that'll drive anyone crazy: that when you see yourself reflected in someone's eyes – as happened to me once – you see a beggar standing at a gate he can never enter. The one who goes in can never be you, in your closed-off, self-created world . . . It's someone you don't know, the one who is seen by the person who looks into your eyes, and his world is closed off from yours. (*Pause.*) It's got dark in here.

Ordulf (*eagerly*) Would you like me to fetch the lamp?

Henry The lamp, yes . . . the lamp. Do you think I don't know that as soon as I turn my back, off to bed with my oil lamp . . . you switch on the lights? – same thing in the throne room. I pretend not to notice.

Ordulf Ah, well, in that case, would you like . . .

Henry No, it's blinding, I want my lamp.

Ordulf Fine – it's right outside.

Ordulf goes out, returning immediately with an antique lamp – one of those you hold by a ring on top.

Henry Good. Shed a little light. Sit there, round the table . . . No, not bolt upright . . . make yourself comfortable . . . And I'll go here . . . Pity we can't order up a nice moonbeam. The moon is our friend. I often feel grateful to her . . . lost to myself, gazing up at her from my window . . . Who would believe that she knows nine hundred and twenty-seven years have gone by and I, sitting at my window like any poor fellow, can't really be Henry IV? I say, what a lovely picture we make: 'The Emperor Among His Faithful Counsellors: Night'. Isn't this nice?

Landolf (*quietly to Bertold*) Do you realise? If we'd only known it was all pretend . . .

Henry What was?

Landolf Er . . . what I mean is . . . this morning I was just saying to him . . . (*He points at Bertold.*) because he's just joined . . . I was saying, what a shame, what with our costumes, and lots more in wardrobe, and with that throne room . . .

Henry What about it? What's a shame?

Landolf Well . . . that we never knew . . .

Henry That this comedy was a farce?

Landolf Because we thought . . .

Harold Yes, that it was all real.

Henry And it isn't? You don't think it's real?

Landolf Well, if you're saying . . .

Henry What I'm saying is that you're all stupid. You should have acted out the make-believe for yourselves, not for my sake or the occasional visitor, but just like this, behaving naturally, with no one to see . . . eating, sleeping, scratching your arse, living, alive in the remote, romantic, sepulchral past, here at the court of Henry IV! And reflecting that nine hundred years on, there are people scuffling about in a permanent state of torment to know how things will turn out for them. While you, meanwhile, are already history! Whatever happens has all happened, however sad my fate, however painful the events and brutal the battles, they're history and nothing can change them, they're fixed, for ever . . . so you can sit back and admire how every cause leads obediently to its effect, with perfect logic, how every event fits neatly with every other. That's the wonderful thing about history.

Landolf Beautiful . . . beautiful . . .

Henry Yes – but now it's over. Now that you're in on it I can't do it any more. I can't take my oil lamp to bed. I'm bored with it all! (*almost to himself, violent with contained anger*) By God, I'll make her sorry she came! Dressed up as my mother-in-law! And that Abbot! Dragging along a doctor to study me. Thought they'd cure me, did they? Idiots! I'd love to give at least one of them a slap – yes, that one, a famous swordsman, I believe. He'll run me through! Well, we'll see, won't we . . .?

There is a knock at the door.

Who is it?

Giovanni (*offstage*) Deo gratis.

Harold Oh, it's Giovanni come to do his evening performance as the little monk!

Ordulf Good, let's make him do the whole thing!

Henry (*sternly*) You're a fool – you don't understand . . . making fun of a poor old man who's only doing this out of love for me.

Landolf (*to Ordulf*) We have to take it seriously, do you see?

Henry Exactly. Deadly serious. Otherwise truth is just a bad joke.

Henry opens the door and lets Giovanni in, dressed as a humble monk, with a parchment scroll under his arm.

Come in, Father. (*continuing to them*) All the documents concerning my life and reign that had anything good to say about me were destroyed by my enemies. Nothing survived except this, my biography, written down by a humble and devoted monk . . . and you'd make fun of him? (*to Giovanni, fondly*) Sit down, Father . . . sit there and . . . keep the lamp by you. (*Henry sets the oil lamp next to Giovanni.*) Ready?

Giovanni (*unrolling the parchment*) Ready, Your Majesty.

Henry So, write . . . (*dictating*) 'Henry, it will be said, was a tragic figure and a national hero for his efforts to maintain a united Germany against the ambitions of the barons. His excommunication gave them their opportunity. On October 16th 1076, at the Diet of Tribur, they decreed that Henry would lose his kingdom if he did not receive absolution within a year and a day. But he escaped to Italy, and at Canossa in January 1077, in the castle of his enemy Matilda of Tuscany, he threw himself on the mercy of the Pope . . . '

Act Three

The throne room is dark. The canvases of the two paintings have been removed and in their place, inside the frames, are Frida, dressed as the 'Countess of Tuscany', as we've seen her in Act Two and Carlo Di Nolli, dressed as 'Henry IV', frozen in the same postures as the paintings. Henry IV enters, holding the lamp.

Frida Henry!

Henry stops at the sound of the voice and turns, frightened.

Henry Who's that?

Frida (*slightly louder*) Henry!

Henry shrieks and drops the oil lamp, puts his arms around his head and makes as if to run away. Frida jumps from the frame yelling like a madwoman.

Henry! Henry! I'm scared!

Matilda, dressed like Frida, enters. Henry sees her and recoils again, shrieking. At the same time Di Nolli jumps down, rushing to Frida, who keeps on screaming, almost fainting.

Di Nolli It's all right, Frida, it's me, I'm here . . .

Matilda, furious, slaps Henry's face.

Matilda Bastard!

Hidden electric lights switch on, illuminating the room in a harsh glare. From the door everybody rushes in: the Doctor, Matilda (dressed as the 'Countess of

56

*Tuscany'), Belcredi, Landolf, Harold, Ordulf, Bertold
and Giovanni. Henry IV stands there watching,
confused. The others, ignoring him, rush to help and
comfort Frida, who is sobbing in the arms of her
fiancé. They are all talking in great confusion.*

Belcredi It's a wrap!

Doctor All over!

Matilda He made fools of us, Frida! Do you see? – he
was cured all along!

Di Nolli Cured?

Belcredi It was all an act. Everything's all right.

Frida I'm so scared!

Matilda There's nothing to be scared of now – look at
him!

Di Nolli What is? What do you mean, cured?

Doctor So it seems, the two-faced . . .

Belcredi That's right – (*pointing to the four counsellors*)
they told us all about it.

Matilda He's been cured for ages – he confessed.

Di Nolli But he's only just – this moment –

Belcredi It was all put on, he was laughing at you up his
sleeve – us, too, for all our pains.

Di Nolli I can't believe it! – Making a fool of his own
sister right up to her death?

*Henry has remained, all hunched up, peeping out at
them. He stands up and shouts at Di Nolli.*

Henry Yes? Keep going! Go on!

Di Nolli (*startled*) Go on what?

57

Henry She wasn't just 'your sister' – was she?

Di Nolli My sister? I said *your* sister – you made her come here to the bitter end dressed up as your mother Agnes!

Henry Don't you mean *your* mother?

Di Nolli *Of course* I mean my mother!

Henry But your mother's been dead for centuries – you've just arrived fresh from there . . . jumping out newborn from your box . . . How do you know I haven't been mourning her for years, in my heart, even dressed as I am?

Matilda What's he talking about?

Doctor Calm down, everyone, please . . .

Henry What am I talking about? I'm asking you, wasn't Agnes the mother of Henry IV? (*turning to Frida*) You should know, Countess, if anyone does.

Frida Me? I don't know anything!

Doctor He's having a relapse – stand back, everyone.

Belcredi Relapse, my eye! He's playing games again.

Henry Me? Who was in the picture frame? – Himself! Henry IV!

Belcredi We've had enough of this joke.

Henry Who said it was a joke?

Doctor Don't provoke him, for God's sake.

Belcredi They did! (*pointing again at the four counsellors*) Them!

Henry You? Did you tell them it was a joke?

Landolf No . . . we just said you were cured.

Belcredi There you are. (*to Matilda*) Aren't you embarrassed at yourself? – Look at him (*indicating Di Nolli*) – look at yourself, Countess – in your fancy dress!

Matilda Oh, shut up! What does it matter who's wearing what, if he's really cured?

Henry Yes, I'm really cured. (*to Belcredi*) But I haven't finished with you yet. (*aggressively*) Are you aware that in twenty years no one has dared to come into my presence dressed like you and this gentleman here? (*He points to the Doctor.*)

Belcredi Of course I am. For that matter, when I appeared before you this morning I came dressed –

Henry – as a monk, of course!

Belcredi You mistook me for Peter Damian, and the only reason I didn't laugh was –

Henry You thought I was crazy. So, now that I'm sane, you can jeer at her to see her in costume? And yet, you might have reflected that, in my eyes, she looks . . . Oh, what does it matter? (*turning suddenly to the Doctor*) You're a doctor?

Doctor Er – yes . . .

Henry So all this was your idea. Don't you realise you could have plunged my mind back into the dark pit of madness . . . making pictures talk and leap out of their frames? (*Henry observes Frida and Di Nolli, then Matilda, and lastly he looks at his own clothes.*) Double, double . . . Splendid, just what the doctor ordered for the lunatic . . . (*pointing at Belcredi*) To him it's just another masquerade. (*addressing Belcredi*) And now – off with the motley, eh? – so I can come along with you – do you think?

59

Belcredi With me – with us . . .

Henry Where should we go, then? How about the club? In best bib and tucker. Or shall we go home with the Countess, the two of us?

Belcredi Whatever you like. Why not? You don't want to stay here – all alone and for evermore – keeping up a carnival joke that went wrong? It's amazing how you managed to keep it going once you'd recovered from the accident.

Henry Ah, yes – but when the horse threw me and I hit my head, I actually did lose my mind, I'm not sure for how long.

Doctor Ah! Most interesting! How long roughly?

Henry About twelve years. (*to Belcredi*) Yes – knowing nothing about what life had in store for you and not for me, from the day of the carnival onwards . . . all the changes, friends who turned against me, or how my place was taken, in . . . let's say . . . the heart of a woman I loved . . . not knowing who'd died, who'd gone away . . . all that, you know, was no joke.

Belcredi That's not what I said – I was talking about later, when . . .

Henry Oh – later! Well, one day . . . Are you listening, Doctor? – I'm a very interesting case, you should take notes . . . Well, one day . . . all by itself, God knows how, the damage here – (*He touches his forehead.*) – mended itself . . . I open my eyes slowly, to begin with I'm not sure if I'm asleep or awake – and then, yes, I'm awake, I touch things, the fog is clearing . . . I'm cured . . . And now – just as he says (*pointing to Belcredi*) – yes, throw off the masquerade! The nightmare! Open the doors and windows! Breathe in the air! Quick! Away! (*more calmly*)

But where? For what? For everybody to point a furtive finger? – 'There goes Henry IV!' And not as you see me now, but out in the world, arm in arm with you, my dear friends!

Belcredi It wouldn't be like that.

Matilda Who'd ever . . . ? It's unthinkable. It was an accident.

Henry They used to say I was cuckoo before I had the accident. (*to Belcredi*) You know that better than anyone – anybody who stuck up for me got an argument from you.

Belcredi Oh, come on, it was all in good heart.

Henry And there's my hair – look.

Belcredi But mine's going grey, too.

Henry Yes, but there's a difference. I turned grey in here, as Henry IV. Can you understand what that means? I didn't realise! – I just noticed it one day, it was a shock, because I knew at once it wasn't just my hair, *I* was going grey, I was rotting away. I was done, I'd missed the feast.

Belcredi You weren't left abandoned . . .

Henry I know. They longed for me to get better. Even the one who was right behind me and jabbed my horse till the blood ran . . .

Di Nolli What?

Henry . . . jabbed it to make it rear up, till it threw me.

Matilda It's the first I've heard of this!

Henry Was that in good heart, too, do you suppose?

Matilda Who? Who was behind us?

Henry What does it matter? It could as well have been any of those who went on to the banquet and would have saved me their meagre leftovers of sympathy, a few bones of contrition on the edge of their plates. Thank you very much!

So, Doctor – see if I'm not a precedent in the annals of lunacy! I decided to stay mad, finding everything I needed here for a completely new form of amusement, to live as a madman of sound mind. Maybe it was to get my own back on the paving stone that cracked my head. What I saw when I came round was solitude, bleak and empty, and I decided to deck it out in all the colours and splendour of that long-gone carnival day when you . . . oh, there you are, My Lady . . . when you had your triumph . . . and to make everyone who came here continue – this time for my diversion – that celebrated masquerade which had been – for you if not for me – just the whim of a day . . . to make it last for ever, not as make-believe now but as the real thing, the genuine mad article: the right clothes, the throne room, the four Privy Counsellors – all of them traitors, I gather – (*turning to them*) I'd like to know what you think you've gained by it? If I'm cured, you're out of a job. I must have been mad to confide in you. But now it's my turn. Guess what? They were thinking we could carry on this charade behind your backs!

Henry begins to laugh. The others, with the exception of Matilda, laugh too.

Belcredi Hear that? Not bad, eh?

Di Nolli Did you?

Henry Don't blame them. (*shaking his clothes*) We are what we wear. Look, this is an obvious, deliberate caricature of that other charade which is the life we live

62

as puppets . . . so you have to forgive them, they don't realise it's only their frocks. (*to Belcredi*) You soon enter into the spirit of it. You start behaving as if you're in some tragedy, like this . . . (*He demonstrates.*) I'm cured, gentlemen, because I've woken up to my madness. So I'm calm. Your problem is you haven't woken up to yours, so you toss and turn your whole lives through.

Belcredi Oh, so in the end, we're the madmen, are we?

Henry Well, if you weren't crazy, would you have shown up here with her?

Belcredi I might if I thought you were crazy.

Henry And what about her?

Belcredi Ah, her . . . I don't know about her. She's hanging on to your every word, she seems quite entranced by your sane-as-a-hatter emergence. (*to Matilda*) Since you're dressed for the part, Countess, why don't you join him?

Matilda Damn your insolence!

Henry Take no notice! – he can't help provoking me, though the Doctor warned him. (*to Belcredi*) Why should I care about what happened between us? – the part you played in my unlucky love . . . (*indicating Belcredi to Matilda*) . . . the part he now plays in your life! My life has been this one here. I wasn't there when you got old. Was that what you wanted to tell me, to show me, by dressing up, stooping to this – on doctor's orders? Nice one, Doctor. 'Before' and 'After', eh? But unfortunately for you, I'm not that crazy. I knew damn well he wasn't Henry IV. Because I'm Henry IV. I've been Henry IV for years . . . stuck behind my mask, while she's lived life and enjoyed herself for twenty years . . . and become – look at her there – someone I don't know any more . . .

63

because I know her like this . . . (*pointing at Frida and moving closer to her*) to me this will always be her. Now you look like children ready to jump out of their skins. (*to Frida*) And you were frightened, weren't you, my sweet, by the game they tricked you into playing? How could you know it wasn't the game they thought it was? Oh, what a marvellous terror! – the dream that comes to life, never more alive than in you. You were only an image but they made you flesh . . . blood . . . breath. You're mine – mine! – mine by right!

Henry takes her in his arms, laughing insanely, while everybody shrieks in terror; but when they rush to pull Frida away from him he becomes menacing and shouts to his four counsellors.

Hold them off! Hold them! I order you!

The four counsellors, stunned, fascinated, automatically try to restrain Di Nolli, the Doctor and Belcredi.

Belcredi Let go of her! Let go! You're no madman!

Henry takes Landolf's sword.

Henry Oh no? (*He runs Belcredi through.*) Are you sure?

Belcredi screams. Everyone rushes to Belcredi's aid, shouting in confusion.

Di Nolli Is it bad?

Bertold Right in the guts!

Doctor I warned you! Didn't I tell you?

Frida Oh my God!

Di Nolli Frida, stay by me.

Matilda He's mad! – Mad!

Di Nolli Hold him down!

Belcredi (*protesting fiercely*) Oh no . . . there's nothing crazy about you! He's not mad! He isn't mad!

They take Belcredi, continuing to yell, out. Among the cries there is a more piercing one from Matilda, followed by silence.
Henry remains onstage, between Landolf, Harold and Ordulf, with his eyes wide open, in astonishment.

Henry Now . . . yes . . . no two ways about it . . . Together again . . . Henry the Fourth, now and for ever.

The End.